Felix Mendelssohn

SYMPHONIES NOS. 3, 4 and 5

in Full Score

From the Breitkopf & Härtel
Complete Works Edition

DOVER PUBLICATIONS, INC.
Mineola, New York

Bibliographical Note

This Dover edition, first published in 2007, is an unabridged republication
of selections from *Felix Mendelssohn Bartholdy's Werke. Kritisch durchgesehene
Ausgabe von Julius Rietz. Mit Genehmigung der Originalverlager,* originally published by Breitkopf & Härtel, Leipzig, between 1874 and 1877.

International Standard Book Number

ISBN-13: 978-0-486-46415-2
ISBN-10: 0-486-46415-6

Manufactured in the United States by Courier Corporation
46415602
www.doverpublications.com

CONTENTS

Symphony No. 3 in A
("Scottish"), Op. 56
Dedicated to Queen Victoria of England

I

Die einzelnen Sätze dieser Symphonie müssen gleich auf einander folgen, und nicht durch die sonst gewöhnlichen längeren Unterbrechungen von einander getrennt werden. Für die Hörer kann der Inhalt der einzelnen Sätze auf dem Programm des Concertes angegeben werden wie folgt: *

Introduction und **Allegro agitato.** — **Scherzo assai vivace.** — **Adagio cantabile.** — **Allegro guerriero** und **Finale maestoso.**

* The movements of this symphony must follow one another immediately, and must not be separated by the customary long pauses. For the listeners, the content of the movements can be indicated on the concert program as follows:

1

attacca

IV

Allegro vivacissimo. ♩= 126.

Symphony No. 4 in A
("Italian"), Op. 90

I

Più animato poco a poco.

III

IV

SALTARELLO.
Presto.

Symphony No. 5
("Reformation") Op. 107

I

Allegro con fuoco.

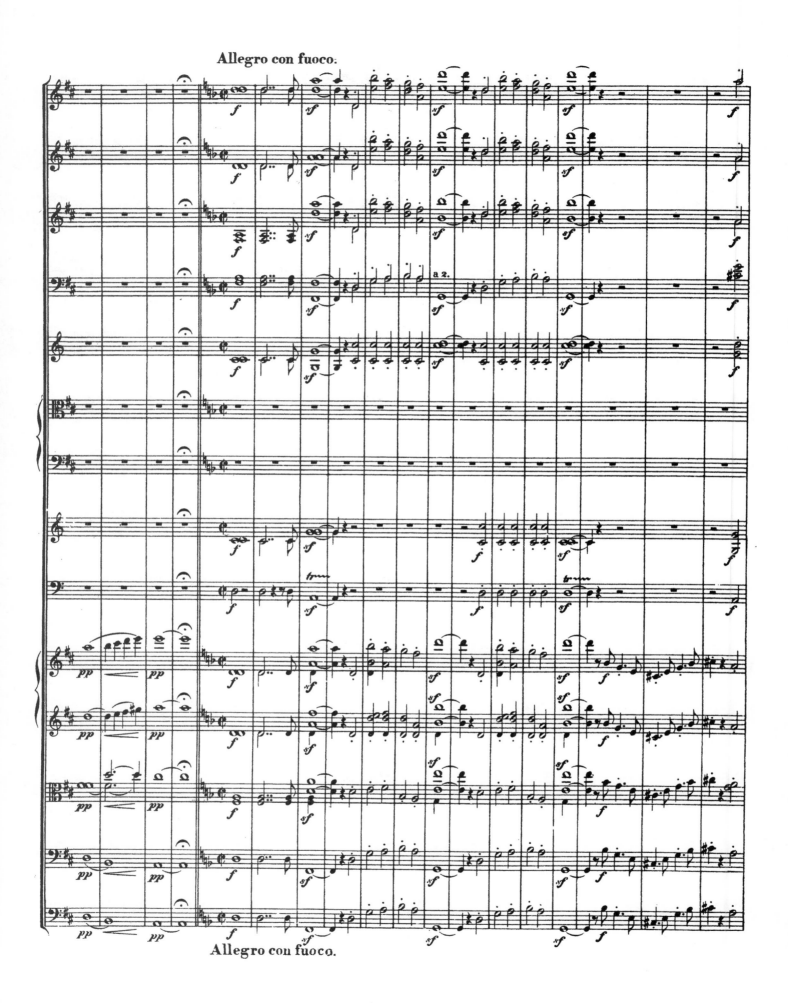

176   *Symphony No. 5, Mvt. I*

Andante come I.   meno Allegro come I.

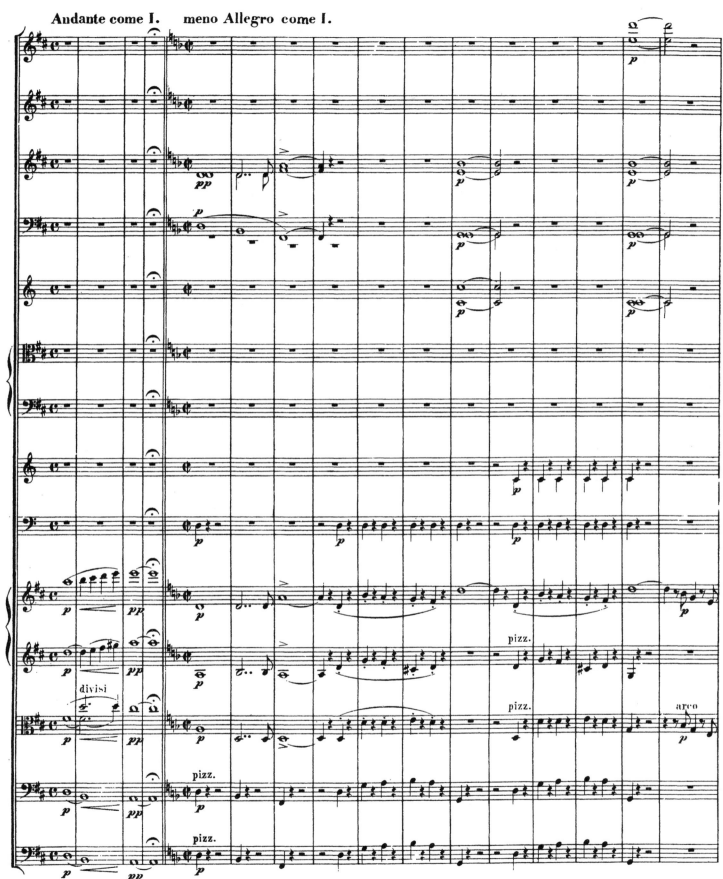

Andante come I.   meno Allegro come I.

II

Allegro vivace.

Flauti.

Oboi.

Clarinetti in B♭.

Fagotti.

Corni in B♭ basso.

Trombe in E♭.

Timpani in D.A.

Violino I.

Violino II.

Viola.

Violoncello.

Basso.

Allegro vivace.

III

Flauti.

Clarinetti in C.

Fagotti.

Corni in D.

Trombe in D.

Timpani in D.A.

Violino I.

Violino II.

Viola.

Violoncello.

Basso.

Andante.

IV

Chorale: *Ein feste Burg ist unser Gott*

Andante con moto.

Andante con moto.

Allegro vivace.

Allegro maestoso.

Allegro maestoso.

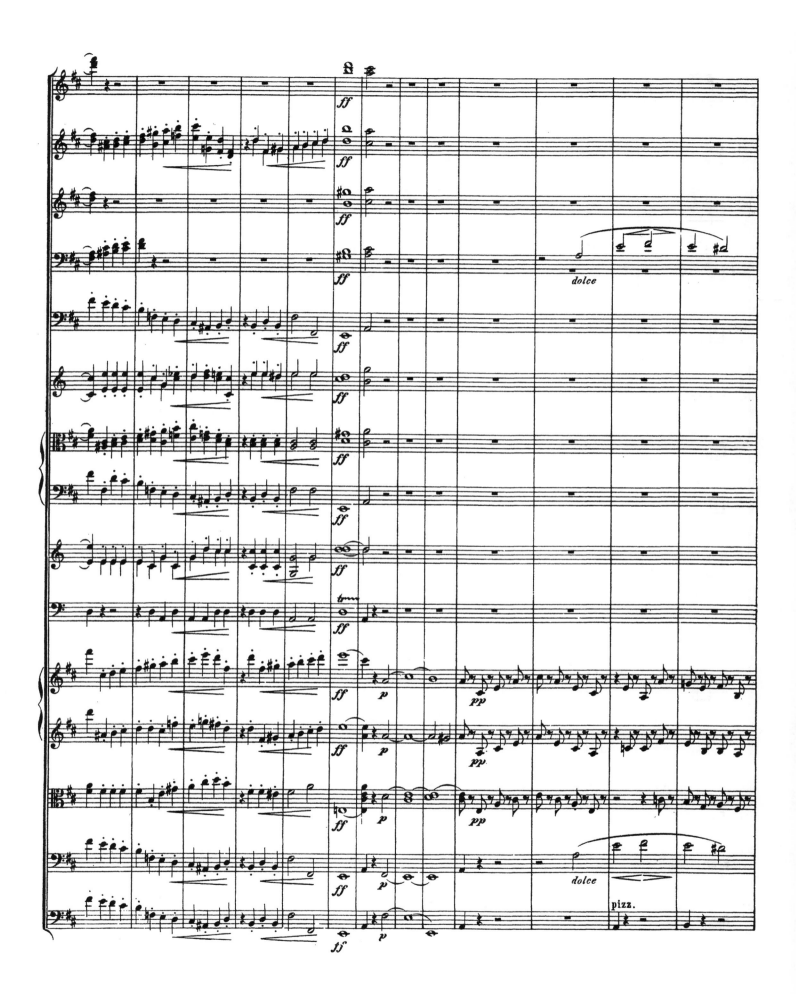

THE END